# The Mourning
# of Our Children

## Brenda Brittain

TRILOGY CHRISTIAN PUBLISHERS

*TUSTIN, CA*

Trilogy Christian Publishers
A Wholly Owned Subsidary of Trinity Broadcasting Network
2442 Michelle Drive
Tustin, CA 92780

*The Mourning of Our Children*

Manufactured in the United States of America

10 9 8 7 6 5 4 3 2 1

Library of Congress Cataloging-in-Publication Data is available.

ISBN: 978-1-68556-607-4

E-ISBN: 978-1-68556-608-1

# Dedication

Every moment in life contributes to the journal we write. Some moments are easy and some are hard, but each one is precious and surprisingly not unique. These are some of my moments, and some are moments many others have shared with me.

To my beloved husband, Joseph, forever standing strong together.

To my very loved sons and daughters, James (J.J.) and Stella, Shad and Kelli, Brandy and Chris and their children, Jayda, Jameson, Sara, Calob, Brandon, and Olivia, and their children and their children, for a thousand generations may His favor be upon you.

This was Mint 2B.

# Acknowledgements

*Oh, give thanks to the Lord, for He is good, for His steadfast love endures forever!*

First and foremost, I must give full honor and acknowledgment to God for the ability, strength, and timing of this book. Words guided by the Holy Spirit and the unceasing love of Jesus Christ. To God be the Glory!

Blessed beyond measure is how I would describe my wonderful and faithful friends. Melissa Ramsay, Shonna Hardin, Amber Wilson, Carolyn Addy, Barbara Wolinski, Kathy Fenhaus, Brooke Dawdy, Janet Wilson, Malisa Espinal, Carmella Culp, and Francis Faz. All faithful disciples of Christ and sisters, forever in my heart.

A special thank you to my church family at Foundation Christian Ministries in Bastrop, Texas. Your enthusiasm for worship, fellowship, service, and discipleship is shown not only within the walls of the church but in the way you project your love for Christ out in the community.

Pastor Chris Pena and Pastor Melissa Pena, your enthusiastic love for God's Word and passionate ways of delivering the Good News through meaningful sermon series, prayer, and worship were what first drew us to choose FCM as our church home. Your bold leadership, contagious smiles, and devotion to teaching us to be Christ-like disciple-makers have been a blessing and inspiration.

Pastor Raquel Pena, your voice, your smile, your passion...You are a gift to all of us at Foundation Christian Ministries.

# Contents

# Silently and Privately

Dear brothers and sisters, whenever trouble comes your way, let it be an opportunity for joy. For when your faith is tested, your endurance has a chance to grow. So let it grow, for when your endurance is fully developed, you will be strong in character and ready for anything.

If you need wisdom—if you want to know what God wants you to do—ask him, and he will gladly tell you. He will not resent you for asking. But when you ask him, be sure that you really expect him to answer...

James 1:2–6 (NLT)

Silently and privately, many of us are mourning our children. No, they are not dead, they are healthy, raising their children, building their careers, and living their lives. But still, we mourn.

Silently and privately, many of us are experiencing extreme guilt for failures we may or may not be guilty of. Failure to have our children actively involved in their faith, working for the Kingdom, living lives that are Scripture-based.

The mere thought of facing Jesus at Believers' Judgment and having Him point out that our children are not there with us is unbearable.

Silently and privately, many of us do not know what our grown children's true relationship is with God, with Jesus, with the Holy Spirit...because when the subject is brought up, we get eye rolls, excuses, and sometimes insults to our zealousness or non-perfection.

So, we mourn silently and privately.

Parents in their forties, fifties, and sixties are facing a relationship dilemma never experienced before on such a massive scale. Throughout history, we have seen children rebel from their parents in a variety of ways, but the current culture taking over today cuts to the bone and hurts more than the simple rebellion of the past.

We mourn the dreams we had of what our relationship with them would be. We mourn the inability to love up our grandchildren. We mourn holidays, shopping trips, vacations, and Sunday dinners. We did our best to raise them with a balance of love and discipline. They are hardworking, well-educated, and socially popular.

But for reasons that we cannot fully grasp, we find ourselves walking on eggshells in their presence. We think we are the only ones. But we are not alone. There is a quiet epidemic spreading through our cities and rural communities. We mourn for our children.

First, this book is not intended for families torn apart by major issues. Child abuse, whether physical, sexual, or emotional, is never acceptable and is a fully and completely justifiable reason for the separation from parents who contributed to, participated in, or looked the other way when the abuse was happening. This book is for "normal" families who lived "normal" lives and conducted themselves in responsible, loving, and supportive ways. Normal, by the way, does not mean free from sin, free from dependency, or free from bad choices.

As parents, we must acknowledge that we are not free from guilt. We messed up...a lot. We listened to bad advice from experts that we saw on talk shows and based our own self-worth on the lives of women who seemed to have it all at the time but now are in rehab or whose facial features have been dramatically altered because they are terrified of growing old. No, we as parents were not perfect, but we tried. We were duped by the media and tried to have it all, which we can have, just not all at once, at the same time.

But we tried...and we dreamed. We wanted Thanksgiving and Christmas, we wanted trips to Disneyland and picnics in the backyard.

But it seems the time we spend with our children is tense and guarded. We have discovered that a well-meaning piece of advice or comment will offend and be turned into something it was not intended to be. We try too hard, and sometimes even try to buy their love, but at the end of each visit feel even more alone than we did on the visit before. And eventually, we give up.

### Silently and Privately, between You and God

Who are you mourning today?

_____

_____

What is your greatest fear or loss at this moment?

_____

_____

_____

_____

# So, Now What?

Do we silently and privately mourn? Beat ourselves up on a daily basis? Cry ourselves to sleep every night? Probably.

As Christians, we search for answers and peace through the Word of God. And once again, He does not let us down. Jesus, in fact, took full responsibility for what was happening as he addressed the crowds.

> I have come to bring fire to the earth, and I wish that my task were already completed! There is a terrible baptism ahead of me, and I am under a heavy burden until it is accomplished!
>
> Do you think I have come to bring peace to the earth? No, I have come to bring strife and division! From now on families will be split apart, three in favor of me, and two against— or perhaps the other way around. There will be a division between father and son,

mother and daughter, mother-in-law and daughter-in-law.

Luke 12:49–53 (TLB)

The division Jesus was speaking to in Luke was in reference to those who would follow Him and those who would choose not to. The enemy, of course, has used these words, twisted them, and expanded upon them to cause strife within families for his own evil plan. Being aware of this misuse of Christ's words and sharing it with family members gives us the opportunity to not fall into Satan's trap and re-think our words and reactions to the words of others.

But then there are those who are choosing to walk away from faith, choosing to allow the strife and division to occur. Then the warning from Jesus stands as truth.

So, does that mean "It is what it is"? If Jesus is telling us that this is the way it will be, is there anything we can do to change it, to alter our destiny?

**Silently and Privately, between You and God**

How do you think the statement in Luke 12:52 has affected your current family relationships?

_____

_____

How can you now change the strife and division using this Scripture verse to relate to others?

_____

_____

_____

# Hope, Faith, Repentance, and Salvation

The one thing I know. The one thing we, as Christians, can count on is hope. Our faith is based on being given the opportunity to change...change ourselves, our lives, our relationships, and our eternity. This is why we don't give up; why Jesus, even after stating that families would be split apart, gave us hope.

Jesus told this parable of hope for change in our lives, one last chance.

> ...A man planted a fig tree in his garden and came again and again to see if there was any fruit on it, but he was always disappointed. Finally, he said to his gardener, "I've waited three years, and there hasn't been a single fig!

Cut it down. It's taking up space we can use for something else."

The gardener answered, "Give it one more chance. Leave it another year, and I'll give it special attention and plenty of fertilization. If we get figs next year, fine. If not, then you can cut it down."

Luke 13:6–9 (NLT)

Special attention and plenty of fertilization, what does that look like? At first glance, you may think that means to pour all you have into your adult children, their wives, and their husbands. But is that what Scripture teaches us?

Consider the parable of the Lost Son in Luke chapter 15. Jesus describes a family of great wealth and accomplishment. One son is hardworking, devoted to his father and the family business. The other son is more of a "free spirit," ready to experience what the world has to offer...on dad's money. Convincing his father to give him his share of the inheritance early, he sets off without regard for his family, the business, his faith, and the teachings and expectations of that faith, and apparently even less for the emotional toll his behavior will bring. And then life happens. The money is gone, the fun is over, and reality sets in. Having no skills, he is forced to work the lowest of jobs just to barely get by.

Hunger and the discovery that all those who were willing to be there in support when his pockets were full have disappeared. A longing to go home, to seek solace from family sets in, but so does Repentance. He suddenly recognizes that his behavior has hurt more than his pride and the hunger inside of him is for more than just food.

> I will go home to my father and say, "Father, I have sinned against both heaven and you, and I am no longer worthy of being called your son. Please take me on as a hired servant."
>
> Luke 15:18–19 (NLT)

Would he have come to the recognition that his behavior was directly impacting his life and relationships if he could have just called up Dad and asked to have some money put on his credit card? How hungry would he have gotten if Mom was restocking his fridge? Would the odor of the pigs have sunk in if someone stopped by regularly and did his laundry or dropped off new clothes because they loved him? Probably not.

As we continue to read in Luke, consider the ways that special attention and fertilization (continued parental support of bad behavior) would have altered the lesson Jesus was giving through the parable:

So he returned home to his father. And while he was still a long distance away, his father saw him coming. Filled with love and compassion, he ran to his son, embraced him, and kissed him. His son said to him, "Father, I have sinned against both heaven and you, and I am no longer worthy of being called your son."

...But his father said to the servants, "Quick! Bring the finest robe in the house and put it on him. Get a ring for his finger, and sandals for his feet. And kill the calf we have been fattening in the pen. We must celebrate with a feast, for this son of mine was dead and has now returned to life. He was lost, but now is found." So the party began.

Luke 15:20–24 (NLT)

With the wrong type of special attention and fertilization, these events in the story would have been altered:

1. The son would not have repented and vowed to change his behavior and expectations.
2. He would not have returned home willingly.
3. The Father's disappointment and frustration would not have changed into being filled with love and compassion.

4. There would have been no embrace, no celebration, no rejoicing.

The lesson on forgiveness would be lost. The teaching is that every soul is worth saving, every person is of value, and every bad decision can become a moment of reconciliation and redemption with time, sometimes one more hour, one more day, one more year.

But it is never that easy when you are a parent. As soon as you have a good relationship with one of your children, one of your sons-in-law, or daughters-in-law somehow, and almost always, there is another who feels slighted. They are fast to point out why they are now justified in being angry with you, and it begins again, different actors, same story.

> Meanwhile, the older son was in the field. When he came near the house, he heard music and dancing. So he called one of the servants and asked him what was going on. "Your brother has come," he replied, "and your father has killed the fattened calf because he has him back safe and sound." The older brother became angry and refused to go in. So, his father went out and pleaded with him. But he answered his father, "Look! All these years I've been slaving for you and

never disobeyed your orders. Yet you never gave me even a young goat so I could celebrate with my friends. But when this son of yours, who has squandered your property with prostitutes comes home, you kill the fattened calf for him."

Luke 15:25–30 (NIV)

And just when he thought his mourning was over, it began again: the eggshell stepping, the explaining of that which should not need to be explained.

His father said to him, "Look, dear son, you and I are very close, and everything I have is yours. We had to celebrate this happy day. For your brother was dead and has come back to life! He was lost, but now he is found!"

Luke 15:31–32 (NLT)

No one told us that once we raised our children, we would get a season pass to the most peace-stealing carnival ever. Whether you are on a roller coaster of ups and downs or the merry-go-round of a never-ending emotional battle, the only way off the ride is through Jesus Christ. Unceasing prayer, learning to separate actual offenses from perceived offenses, and learning the art of discernment before responding in the flesh are required to recapture your peace.

> And the peace of God, which transcends all understanding, will guard your hearts and your minds in Christ Jesus.
>
> Philippians 4:7 (NIV)

**Silently and Privately, between You and God**

As you look forward with hope, how do you think you can give special attention and fertilization to your situation, without causing further harm?

_____

_____

_____

_____

# Prayer Time

*Most gracious Heavenly Father,*

*You know the deepest hurts in our hearts, the hurts we cannot speak of because our voices can't. You know the depth of love and devotion we have for you, for our families, for our children. No matter how hard our relationships seem to be, we cling to the promise of the family, the family you made, you created. There is comfort in knowing that we are not alone. The times when we feel defeated, we are reminded that you removed that defeat from us on the cross. Your selfless love for us keeps us going, keeps us determined to bring our families to you. We pray, dearest Lord, for your grace, peace, blessings, and wisdom. And we look forward with great anticipation to the day we also "celebrate this happy day" with you.*

*In Jesus' most Holy Name. Amen.*

# Okay, Time to Stand Up, Seriously, Stand Up!

Stand up tall, remember whose child you are, straighten your crown. You are the child of the Most High God.

> Yet to all who did receive him, to those who believed his name, he gave the right to become children of God.
>
> John 1:12 (NIV)

His plan for you as a parent was not to focus on the things you have little or no control over. All we can do is what we have been directed to do through Scripture. If you have already done these things, do them again. If you have left gaps, fill them in. If you never started, get started.

As I said before, the biggest fear we as believers have, is to be face to face with Jesus at the Believers' Judgment and that He would point out that our children are not there with us.

What we do before this meeting is crucial. Of course, it would be nice to have all the other things, like holidays without eggshells all over the floor, but our focus must be on the Kingdom.

> Let the words of Christ, in all their richness, live in your hearts and make you wise. Use his words to teach and counsel each other. Sing psalms and hymns and spiritual songs to God with thankful hearts. And whatever you do or say, let it be as a representative of the Lord Jesus, all the while giving thanks through him to God the Father.
>
> Colossians 3:16–17 (NLT)

So, as you stand here, know these truths:

You were chosen to be the child of the Most High God. You were chosen.

You were chosen to be the parent of your child. You were chosen.

You were chosen to be in the lives of your stepchildren, in the lives of your daughters and sons-in-law. You were chosen.

This was not a mistake or an act of fate, and it is not more than you can handle. You were chosen for this journey. It may not be easy, it may not even end well, but as you stand face to face with Jesus at Believers' Judgement, your faithfulness in telling your children about the Salvation through Jesus Christ is what will be judged.

> Tell your sons about it, And let your sons tell their sons, And their sons the next generation.
> Joel 1:3 (NASB)

Of all the things you may choose to step away from doing, of all the things you decide to let go, of all the things you decide are not worth the fight over, this is not one. You can be subtle, you can be discreet—at times— but there will be a moment when you must stand up and straighten your crown and declare that your biggest fear is facing eternity without them and that this is not and will never be acceptable to you. You will fight for them; you will stand your ground. Let's take a moment here to look at the Believers' Judgement as relayed to us by John in the Book of Revelation:

And the books were opened, including the
Book of Life. And the dead were judged according to the things written in the books, according to what they have done.

Revelation 20:12 (NLT)

*The Message* Bible says it this way, "And books were
opened. Then another book was opened: the Book of
Life. The dead were judged by the way they had lived."

Remembering that this is not the judgment of non-
believers, who are to face those things that they have
done against God's Word and not accepting the salvation through Jesus Christ, but a look into how believers
lived. What did they do during their lifetime on earth
to further the Kingdom? We were commissioned (instructed) to go and make disciples...this is what will be
reviewed, and our true relationship with Jesus will be
our shining glory.

So, if our biggest fear is standing before Christ and
not having our children there, or maybe just not knowing if they are there or not...we have one job. Don't put
this job off until things are settled and are better.

Preach the Word of God. Be persistent,
whether the time is favorable or not. Pa-
tiently correct, rebuke, and encourage your
people with good teaching. For a time is com-

ing when people will no longer listen to right teaching. They will follow their own desires and will look for teachers who will tell them whatever they want to hear. They will reject the truth and follow strange myths.

2 Timothy 4:2–4 (NLT)

### Silently and Privately, between You and God

Are you willing to have a conversation with your child (children) about your fears regarding their Salvation?

_____

_____

Are you ready to talk to them about your failures or hesitancy over the years to make these things a priority in your relationship with them?

_____

_____

How do you anticipate this conversation will get received and how can your attitude improve this?

_____

_____

_____

_____

_____

# In the Beginning

Never has a truer song verse been written as the one sung by Maria to the Von Camp children in "The Sound of Music": "Let's start at the very beginning, a very good place to start" (Genesis).

The very first mom and the very first dad had the very first children who...well, let's just say, were less than what they probably envisioned for their family. Adam and Eve were definitely less than perfect (as are we).

Their sons, Cain and Abel, had every opportunity to please the Lord, to let their lives be a blessing to their parents. Even without the influence of Facebook, YouTube, and TikTok, Cain managed to insult God and whine about it. Commit the ultimate transgression within a family and then complain about his punishment.

Was Eve to blame for her son's behavior? Well..yes, in the big picture, she did commit the first sin. And Adam, as head of the household, surely had learned a vital lesson and fully recognized the difference between good and evil.

Surely, he learned the consequences that result from those differences at the very moment he was banished from the Garden of Eden. One must assume this lesson was taught to their sons from childhood, but as we all have learned, not all will listen to the lessons their parents try to teach.

When the mere mention of faith, church, Jesus, salvation, grace, anything related to God is rejected and belittled, when you are accused of being overbearing and pushy, and you are told the mere fact that you extended a simple invitation to attend a church event was offensive; remember, you are in good company. Jesus was rejected by His friends, family, hometown, and finally, His disciples.

> And they were deeply offended and refused to believe in him.
>
> Matthew 13:57 (NLT)

> The entire town came out to meet Jesus, but they begged him to go away and leave them alone.
>
> Matthew 8:34 (NLT)

> Jumping up, they mobbed him and forced him to the edge of the hill on which the city was built. They intended to push him over the

cliff, but he slipped away through the crowd and left them.

Luke 4:29–30 (NLT)

Peter swore, "A curse on me if I'm lying— I don't know the man!" And immediately the rooster crowed. Suddenly, Jesus' words flashed through Peter's mind: "Before the rooster crows, you will deny me three times..." And he went away, weeping bitterly.

Matthew 26:74–75 (NLT)

Knowing that even Christ was rejected by those he loved and trusted doesn't make it easier. Trying to figure out how to take the instructions he gave to the disciples when that rejection happens and to follow those instructions within your children's home is no easy task.

When you are invited into someone's home, give it your blessing. If it turns out to be a worthy home, let your blessings stand; if it is not, take back the blessing. If a village doesn't welcome you or listen to you, shake off the dust of that place from your feet as you leave.

Matthew 10:12–14 (NLT)

But then...here comes hope again. That never give up attitude.

But you should keep a clear mind in every
situation. Don't be afraid of suffering for
the Lord. Work at bringing others to Christ.
Complete the ministry God has given you.

2 Timothy 4:5 (NLT)

Re-read that last part: "God has given you." You were
chosen to be the mom, the dad, the mother-in-law, father-in-law, stepmom, stepdad...oh, and don't forget,
chosen to be the child of the Most High God.

We are also told that we will suffer. There is nothing on this earth that could happen to us as parents
that would make us suffer more, make our hearts hurt
more than having an emotional, spiritual, and physical separation from our children. But we are instructed
that even through this suffering, we are to keep a clear
mind in every situation. When your child is believing
the things the world is telling them, you are to keep a
clear mind.

And you must love the Lord your God with all
your heart, all your soul, all your mind, and all
your strength.

Mark 12:30 (NLT)

- Suffering: check
- Rejected: check
- Chosen: check
- Clear mind: working on it.

## Silently and Privately, between You and God

Have you kept a clear mind during the times of rejection from your adult child?

_____

_____

How did your emotions overshadow and contribute to this rejection, lending the same feeling of rejection to your adult child from you?

_____

_____

_____

_____

_____

# Life is Neither a Reality TV Show Nor a Hallmark Movie

As we look at our relationships with our adult children, it is easy to allow the emotions of the moment to write the script for our everyday life. We must stop dwelling on the possibility that we are about to be voted off the island. Trying to stay on the balance beam to keep the immunity idol and make other tribe members content only wears us out physically and emotionally. (You can use your favorite reality show analogy. I'm a *Survivor* fan.)

On the other hand, don't have expectations of having a Hallmark Christmas Movie. Everyone sitting around the perfectly decorated living room sipping Cocoa and talking about everything from old friends to how much they appreciate Grandma's turkey dressing is not going to happen. No matter how much time you put into decorating, cooking, planning, and being joyful…for some reason, the unity will not be there. Maybe because the people sitting on your couch were not hired to be there based on having a perfect smile, and writers are not controlling every conversation.

But don't give up on the vision of sitting with people you love dearly, laughing, sharing what is in your heart, and knowing that they love you back completely.

The thing I have found, very recently, in fact, is having a group of friends, real friends, the kind I now have, is the best thing you can do for yourself. You will be best served to find these friends in a Bible-based, scripturally sound church. Spending time with others who honestly love Jesus and meeting together regularly in study of the Word is a really strong foundation to build friendships on. What will probably amaze you, as it did me, is discovering that many of them are also silently and privately mourning their children.

I can't tell you how often I have started this book, put it away, started it again, put it away. You see, there is one thing that will absolutely happen when it is completed, and the pages are open for the "world" to see. I expect my offenses to be loudly and openly expressed to me. No more silently and privately, and probably all offended at the same time. But I will bear that cross because I know there are so many moms and dads out there that feel alone and isolated. And with that knowledge and being led at this time by the Holy Spirit, it will not be put away again.

There are times when we will have to endure being separated from our families, but we do not have to be alone during these times. Surrounding yourself with friends who know the hurt you are feeling and will pray for you, pray with you, pray over you will make it bearable. And when they know that you will do the same for them, it makes their hurts bearable. The friends turn into family, the silent and private is released and is replaced by love and laughter and new memories.

We are not replacing our family, our children; we are just allowing ourselves to be with people who want and need to be with us right now.

Here is an interesting fact. Our children will be in our place in just a few years. They will be getting the eye rolls, the mean little remarks, the moments of impatience, rudeness, and inconsideration. I remember hearing that you teach people how to treat you. I don't remember treating my parents in this way, in any way that was not respectful, but what a different world we live in. When the influencers (and there were influencers way before TikTtok and social media) started putting out the thoughts of the New Age as a lifestyle, we can trace the self-destruction of respect for others. It became "all about me," caring for yourself first, career above family, quitting a marriage was promoted as a good thing, and children going back and forth between homes normal. Parents and grandparents were suddenly a burden instead of a treasure, and all advice from anyone who was not known by one name or was over the age of forty was dismissed as unenlightened.

I said earlier that I had started writing this book years ago and had put it away. Today, many years after I wrote the first paragraph, the relationship with my older ones is coming around. It was not easy, and it involved stepping back, but never away. It involved loving from afar, but not too far. It involved their own children growing into teens and young adults. It is not where I want it to be yet, for I still do not know if they have accepted Christ...that conversation still gets dismissed. But we can now enjoy time together, phone calls, and the eggshells are few and far between. Noticed I said, "Older ones."

So, if you teach people how to treat you, maybe we were too easy. "Yes, ma'am," and "Yes, sir" became rarer and rarer. Chores were limited and were attached to an allowance, which was given even if the chores weren't done. Our guilt over the hours we worked resulted in our being more interested in being friends than parents, and it was easier to ignore the behaviors that would have caused "bodily harm" if we had done/said them to our parents. But, if you teach people how to treat you by example, what example are our grandchildren seeing of how you treat your parents once you are an adult.

The last couple of years have brought upon us behavior that only four years ago would have been totally unacceptable. I personally find it cruel and heartless, even when done with the best intentions. *What was this shocking behavior done worldwide?* The separation of families from senior members to "keep them safe," leaving them without loving contact, alone, and often on their own. Many elderly people already feel they are a burden, they take on the un-earned guilt of having done something wrong, and a fear of dying alone is all-consuming. The ease in which we, as a society, allowed ourselves to shut down, close the doors on the churches, and not visit those who would have walked through fire for us when we were young is beyond comprehension. Nursing homes denied family visitation, and out of fear and political correctness, that was okay. Those who were already suffering from dementia or were not keeping up with the news never understood why they were no longer seeing family, and those who have lived through some the history's worst days and do not live by fear have said, "Why would I want to live one more year alone when I could live one-week hugging by grandchild and seeing the face of my child?" What example have we set for the next generation? Self- preservation is not what we are told to live for.

Whether young ones are watching their parents be rude and dismissive or watching grandparents left alone and emotionally abandoned, for whatever reason or justification, they are being taught how to treat others.

*All Scripture is inspired by God and is useful to teach us what is true and to make us realize what is wrong in our lives. It straightens us out and teaches us to do what is right. It is God's way of preparing us in every way, fully equipped for every good thing God wants us to do.*

Yes, time flies quickly, and a change needs to happen soon, or this book will need another printing for our kids to read when they are silently and privately.

## Silently and Privately, between You and God

Do you have a person, or a group of people—other than your spouse or other children—to spend time with, who will listen, give honest Scripture-based advice and pray with you?

_____

_____

Knowing that keeping up a false sense of being fine, is not scripturally sound. What do you need to share with them that you have been keeping quiet about?

_____

_____

_____

_____

_____

What behaviors do you recognize that you have that contribute to the issues you now have with your adult children or that influence your responses to their hurtful behaviors or words?

_____

_____

_____

# The Warrior, the Nurturer, and the Onlooker

The following is just a snapshot of some of the relationship issues between children and their parents. One thing that may be helpful as you try to discover why your family is in "eggshell walking" mode is to identify the individual character traits of all involved. I think there are three basic types: the warrior, the nurturer, and the onlooker.

The warrior: always ready to right wrongs, solve problems, fight for truth and justice, is not one to remain complacent or just sit around while life goes on. They will protect those they love and those they have never met. Bold, confident, brave, and tireless.

The nurturer: always compassionate and understanding, tirelessly takes care of physical and emotional needs of others, such as feeding, nursing, comforting, encouraging, and loving. They support and work to teach ways to change poor behaviors that keep others from flourishing.

The onlooker: readily accepts the security given by the warrior and the support given by the nurturer with little regard to the needs or feelings of the warrior and nurturer. They often live their lives based upon their wants and expectations of how they want others to treat them with little active participation in the process of building relationships.

One person may have two or three of these traits, depending on the situation or who they are interacting with. When two traits, such as warrior and nurturer, are combined in all situations, you may find someone who doesn't back down in making sure their focus person is taken care of, whether they want it or not. An onlooker can be the cause of frustration because a lack of action, passion, and energy is not something a warrior can understand. Knowing your traits is key to discovering the traits of others. But, no matter what your character trait, you are given this firm instruction:

> Use every piece of God's armor to resist the enemy in the time of evil, so that after the battle you will still be standing firm. Stand your ground, putting on the sturdy belt of truth and the body armor of God's righteousness.

For shoes, put on the peace that comes from the Good News, so that you will be fully prepared. In every battle, you will need faith as your shield to stop the fiery arrows aimed at you by Satan. Put on salvation as your helmet, and take the sword of the Spirit, which is the word of God. Pray at all times and on every occasion in the power of the Holy Spirit. Stay alert and be persistent in your prayers for all Christians everywhere.

Ephesians 6:13–18 (NLT)

## Silently and Privately, between You and God

Which trait do you instantly recognize yourself to be?

_____

_____

_____

_____

# Samples, Examples, and Sound Familiar

*The Mother-Daughter Relationship*

In the year 597, these words were used in a prophetic message to the Jewish exiles in Babylon.

> Everyone who quotes proverbs will quote this proverb about you: "Like mother, like daughter."
>
> Ezekiel 16:44 (NIV)

This saying can be used as a compliment or a curse. For instance, Paul refers to two women of God whom he admired greatly. In his Second Letter to Timothy, he writes:

I know that you sincerely trust the Lord, for
you have the faith of your mother, Eunice, and
your grandmother, Lois.

2 Timothy 1:5 (NLT)

What do we know about Eunice and Lois? Luke wrote
a short note in his introduction of Timothy in the Book
of Acts using this description:

...There they [Paul and Silas] met Timothy,
a young disciple whose mother was a Jewish believer, but whose father was a Greek.
Timothy was well thought of by the believers
in Lystra and Iconium, so Paul wanted him to
join them on their journey.

Acts 16:1–3 (NLT)

A Jewish woman married to a Greek man was looked
down upon by the Jewish community, and this probably explains why Timothy was not circumcised, as was
the custom. But as we read on in 2 Timothy, Paul gives
credit for Timothy's knowledge of Scripture to learning
it from childhood.

But you must remain faithful to the things
you have been taught. You know they are true,
for you know you can trust those who taught

you. You have been taught the holy Scriptures from childhood, and they have given you the wisdom to receive the salvation that comes in trusting Christ Jesus.

2 Timothy 3:14–15 (NLT)

The mother-daughter team of Lois and Eunice, because of a strong bond of faith, were recognized as the reasons Timothy became one of the first second-generation Christians, a strong man of faith. Like mother, like daughter, in this context, is definitely a compliment.

On the curse end of the spectrum are Herodias and her daughter, also named Herodias. Herodias (mother) was enraged and wanted vengeance on John the Baptist for telling Herod (her husband and king) that their marriage was illegal. King Herod respected John and kept John protected:

Herodias's chance finally came when it was Herod's birthday, and he gave a party for his high government officials, army officers, and the leading citizens of Galilee.

Then his daughter, also named Herodias, came in and performed a dance that greatly pleased them all. "Ask me for anything you like," the king said to the girl, "and I will give it to you." Then he promised, "I will give you whatever you ask, up to half of my kingdom!" She went out and asked her mother, "What should I ask for?" Her mother told her, "Ask for John the Baptist's head!" So, the girl hurried back to the king and told him, "I want the head of John the Baptist, right now, on a tray!"

Mark 6:21–25 (NLT)

So, it would appear that daughters follow the lead of their mothers, but not always. These are the only two examples of mother-daughter relationship in the Bible. Two absolute extremes. Most of us live somewhere in the middle. Trying to be a good example, but having some bad traits and actions jump in when we least expect it. Hoping our daughters won't notice our shortcomings, but they do; hoping our daughters won't notice our faults and sinful ways, but they will. Hoping the good outweighs the bad, the love outweighs the misjudgments, the homemade cookies outweigh the burnt toast, but it often seems they only remember the burnt toast.

While the most complex in its make-up, the easiest to explain and understand is the mother-daughter relationship when it goes astray. It starts at about age nine and is a constant up/down, love/hate, way too different/ way too alike relationship.

As your daughter grows up from that perfect little girl with a ponytail and infectious laugh, all the attributes you dislike about yourself will poke through and will be magnified in her. She, on the other hand, will seek out every available thing you will find objectionable, from clothes to friends, and will know where all your buttons are, how to push them, and how often.

But just because you have gotten used to the ups and downs doesn't make them easier to live through.

*The Father-Daughter Relationship*

Daddy's little girl, all grown up and at times unrecognizable. A sudden disconnect from the person who used to find every way possible to be in his arms, to help him with chores, and to share little secrets. A dad is a natural protector and provider, and when the disconnect is related to a bad choice in boyfriend, husband, friends, or job/life choice, it is hard on a man's heart.

The most heart-wrenching example of a father-daughter relationship in the Bible is the story of Jephthah of Gilead. Making a vow to the Lord:

> "If you give me victory over the Ammonites, I will give to the Lord the first thing coming out of my house to greet me when I return in triumph. I will sacrifice it as a burnt offering."

When Jephthah returned home to Mizpah
[after his victory over the Ammonite army],
his daughter [his only child] ran out to meet
him, playing on a tambourine and dancing
for joy. When he saw her, he tore his clothes
in anguish. "My daughter!" he cried out. "My
heart is breaking! What a tragedy that you
came out to greet me, for I have made a vow
to the Lord and cannot take it back."

Judges 11:30–35 (NLT)

Imagine his anguish in realizing his choice to make
a vow to the Lord and his integrity in keeping that vow
would cost him his daughter. The insight into this type
of father-daughter relationship during this time in history is rare. The information that she was his only child
and that he exclaimed that his heart was breaking when
he realized she was the first to greet him indicates that
they had a close, loving bond. Daughters usually were
more of a commodity and not spoken of in this manner.
Her greeting him by dancing for joy lets us know love
went both ways.

This anguish had to be multiplied by her loving willingness to not only abide by the conditions of his vow
but to seem proud of his victory in battle that the Lord
gave him.

The Apostle Paul wrote a letter to the church in
Philippi to thank them for a gift. His letter included

a plea that two women he was very familiar with and who he had worked with in the church at Philippi to settle their disagreement. No greater gift is given to a dad than a daughter, and nothing is worse than a disagreement tearing apart family, usually over something insignificant or a misunderstanding. Paul, in his wisdom, says not to worry. This is not an easy task for a dad, as he watches the relationship with his daughter go astray, especially if it also includes her relationship with her Heavenly Father also.

> Do not worry about anything, but in everything by prayer and supplication with thanksgiving let your requests be made known to God. And the peace of God, which surpasses all understanding, will guard your hearts and your minds in Christ Jesus.
>
> Philippians 4:6–7 (NRSV)

*The Mother-Son Relationship*

There is a very firm bond between mother and son that just can't be explained. From the time they are babies, little boys love to snuggle, confide, tell their moms everything, and gleefully tease their moms. As they grow into the teen years, there are struggles and disagreements, but generally, the relationship stays firm and active.

Consider the story of Moses' mother, Jochebed, as an example of the love of a mother for her son.

Then Pharaoh gave this order to all his people: "Throw all the newborn Israelite boys into the Nile River. But you may spare the baby girls."

Exodus 1:22 (NLT)

Now a man of the tribe of Levi married a Levite woman, and she became pregnant and gave birth to a son. When she saw that he was a fine child, she hid him for three months. But when she could hide him no longer, she got a papyrus basket for him and coated it with tar and pitch. Then she placed the child in it and put it among the reeds along the bank of the Nile. His sister stood at a distance to see what would happen to him.

Exodus 2:1–4 (NIV)

Soon after this, one of the Pharoah's daughters came down to bathe in the river, and her servant girls walked along the riverbank. When the princess saw the little basket among the reeds, she told one of her servant girls to get it for her. As the princess opened it, she found the baby boy. His helpless cries touched her heart. "He must be one of the Hebrew children," she said.

Then the baby's sister approached the princess. "Should I go and find one of the Hebrew women to nurse the baby for you?" she asked.

"Yes, do!" the princess replied. So the girl rushed home and called the baby's mother. "Take this child home and nurse him for me," the princess told her. "I will pay you for your help." So the baby's mother took her baby home and nursed him.

Later, when he was older, the child's mother brought him back to the princess, who adopted him as her son. The princess named him Moses, for she said, "I drew him out of the water."

Exodus 2:5–10 (NLT)

Jochebed loved her son and risked her life to hide and then save him. Her reward for this love was getting to raise him for many years, teaching him about his Jewish heritage and faith. Then, she further demonstrated that love by letting go of him and allowing him to lead a life that would eventually shape the world.

The most common division in the mother-son bond is another type of love, another type of bond. This new love is usually looked forward to, blessed, and welcomed but often ends in tears: the daughter-in-law.

For this reason, a man will leave his father
and mother and be united to his wife, and the
two will become one flesh.

Ephesians 5:31 (NIV)

The keyword in this verse, and as it is originally stated in Genesis 2:24, is "leave." Most moms want to see their sons leave the nest. We want them to leave willfully, joyfully, eagerly, in anticipation of a new life, new family, new job. Scripture does not say the wife is to take her husband away from his family. It does not provide for her to manipulate her husband, to be jealous of his family bonds, to set boundaries for his relationship with his parents. All too often, the anticipation of a son leaving and becoming his own man is replaced with a son becoming estranged from family, diminished in his position as head of the household, and lost in his faith. The hardest part is often watching your strong son of faith not lead his new family but follow the directions of his wife and fall away from being the man you raised.

*The Father-Son Relationship*

Perhaps the most complex relationship is one between a father and his son. As little boys, sons look up to their dads as their heroes and role model. Dads are the bravest, strongest, "my dad can beat up your dad" persons in the whole world.

Dads often live out their dreams through their sons, visions of being the baseball MVP or the football quarterback who wins the big game. Hours spent on camping trips, practice fields, fixing cars, and building LEGOs is an investment in their sons that no price can be placed.

And then it happens, the boy discovers his dad isn't perfect, and Dad discovers his son is no longer interested in spending time with him or hearing any words of wisdom he has to say.

Even the words of Solomon, the wise King who wrote under God's inspiration, are not heard.

> My children, listen to me. Listen to your father's instruction. Pay attention and grow wise, for I am giving you good guidance. Don't turn away from my teaching. For I, too, was once my father's son, tenderly loved by my mother as an only child.
>
> Proverbs 4:1–3 (NLT)

The parable of the Lost Son in Luke 15 gave us a picture of the relationship between two sons and a dad. One listened and was devoted; one was self-absorbed and foolish. Both ended up in conflict with their father. We know the foolish son repented, returned, and was forgiven. We don't, however, know how the devoted son reacted to his father's explanation:

> His father said to him, "Look, dear son, you and I are very close, and everything I have is yours. We had to celebrate this happy day. For your brother was dead and has come back to life. He was lost, but now he is found!"
>
> Luke 15:31–32 (NLT)

The parable ends there. Maybe that is a lesson itself, learning to not have an expectation that all conflict will end in a celebration. Not knowing the end of the story right away. Just having faith that King Solomon was accurate once again when he wrote:

> Start children off on the way they should go, and even when they are old they will not turn from it.
>
> Proverbs 22:6 (NIV)

But then there is testosterone. When both father and son are natural warriors, there is the need to be "right." They seem to be able to argue, even when they both agree on what they are arguing about.

They are at times just like young goats, someone has to be king of the haystack, and they take turns butting each other off the top and keep returning for the challenge. Each one thinking the other is not respecting or hearing their point of view. They dig in deeper and then hurt feelings are the only winners of this match.

*The Mother-Father-Stepchild Relationship*

Take all of the above relationship information and analysis, mothers, fathers, daughters, sons, and stir into the equation some or all of these factors: another set of parents, past unknown hurts, emotions, fears, disappointments, broken promises, resentment, jealousy, extended families and stereotypical media influences.

There is one main stepparent figure in the Bible. Joseph. Imagine the pressure he was living under. How do you teach your son the trade of being a Carpenter when His Father made the tree? How do you teach him to swim when He can walk on water? Joseph was identified as Jesus' earthly father. He loved Him, taught Him, played with Him, cared for Him, facing more challenges than any of us ever will and doing it with grace.

Most of the stepparents I know, and from my personal experience, your spouses' children are your children. Granted, this is not always the case, but if you are mourning a relationship with this adult child, then we must assume that your heart is wholly vested in them. You have loved them, taken care of them, prayed for them. You have lived the role of teacher, cook, nurse, chauffeur, counselor, travel agent, and the list goes on and on. The hurt is the same no matter what the origination of the parent-child relationship. When other adults and emotions that maybe didn't even involve you are added in, the harder it may be to work through the pain, but you must never forget the fig tree.

> Praise the Lord! How good it is to sing praises to our God! How delightful and how right! The Lord is rebuilding Jerusalem and bringing the exiles back to Israel. He heals the brokenhearted, binding up their wounds. He counts the stars and calls them all by name.
>
> Psalm 147:1–4 (NLT)

*The Mother-Daughter-in-law Relationship*

Whether someone is officially designated as a daughter-in-law or classified in the girlfriend arena, no one seems to have more power over your son. For this book, all young ladies involved in a long-term relationship will be referred to as daughter-in-law, whether they have taken vows or not.

For most mothers of a son, the idea of them falling in love and giving you a daughter-in-love is a welcome dream. Many times, the relationship is pleasant at the beginning, and the anticipation of visits, the joining of families, and future grandchildren is so exciting.

The very loving and devoted relationship between Ruth and her mother-in-law, Naomi, is our inspiration. Naomi was encouraging her widowed daughter-in-law to return to their own families rather than going on the trip to her homeland in search of food and support.

> But Ruth replied, "Don't ask me to leave you and turn back. I will go wherever you go and live wherever you live. Your people will be my people, and your God will be my God."
>
> Ruth 1:16 (NLT)

Ruth's actions did not go unnoticed, and her world changed because of her kind heart. Boaz replied, "But I also know about the love and kindness you have shown your mother-in-law since the death of your husband."

This is the type of mother and daughter-in-law relationship we all hoped for, prayed for, but far too often, the relationship is marred by control issues, jealousy, old baggage, and a lack of confidence. Sometimes these are on the part of the son's wife, and sometimes, if we are to be honest, on the part of the mom. But either way, allowing little things to fester or getting a spirit of offense is a guarantee that life will change, for the worse, very quickly.

To further complicate matters, you must remember that your new "daughter" has a mom of her own, and that relationship can influence your relationship with her. A frequent problem is when "her mom" is jealous of "his mom." Making sure you don't "one-up" each other is key in dealing with your child's new family.

One day, you are enjoying each other, peacefully growing as family and friends, and then, without warning, you are just treated differently, and you don't even know what happened. Conversations cease, visits become tense, grandkids are used as pawns in a chess game that you didn't have any intention of playing. And what hurts even more than having that newly welcomed, new daughter turn on you is watching your loving son become someone you really can't recognize. No longer the strong head of his household, but someone who will just go along to keep peace with his wife, or even worse, turn on you too.

And, if that isn't bad enough, if you have more than one child, you can be dragged into disagreements between siblings and their wives or husbands, and you don't even know what it is all about. But somehow, you end up the bad guy, and if you defend one against the other, even if it is obvious who is right and who is wrong or if you try to stay out of the fray and just try to get everyone in the same room, sitting around that home-cooked meal that includes everyone's favorite dish, you

just may find yourself the only one in the room not being spoken to. Privately and silently, you mourn your
children.

*The Father-Daughter-in-law Relationship*

This relationship is usually good, at least cordial, until the father is forced to watch his family in turmoil and
the common factor is the new daughter he welcomed to
his family. If eye-rolling and rudeness are the issues, it
does hit Dad as hard to take, and if grandchildren are in
the middle of the mess, it makes it much harder.

The prophet Micah gave the same message we received in Matthew and Luke, so again, we must recognize that sometimes relationships are just hard.

> Don't trust anyone—not your best friend or
> even your wife! For the son despises his father.
> The daughter defies her mother. The daugh-
> ter-in-law defies her mother-in-law. Your en-
> emies will be right in your own household.
> Micah 7:5–6 (NLT)

So, where do you go from here?

As for me, I look to the Lord for his help. I
wait confidently for God to save me, and my

God will certainly hear me. Do not gloat over me, my enemies! For though I fall, I will rise again. Though I sit in darkness, the Lord himself will be my light.

Micah 7:7–8 (NLT)

In this relationship, the chance that a conversation regarding the problem will probably not happen...at least one on one. More than likely, a father will talk to his son to try to come to a place of peace. This is a great time for setting an example of being the leader of the family, but this opportunity of often lost when tempers flare or defense mechanisms set in.

*The Mother-Son-in-law Relationship*

This one is usually very dependent on how close you are to your daughter. One of the biggest hardships is when you are the sounding post and shoulder to cry on when they are having issues in their relationship, and yet you are expected to not remember anything said bad against your new son when they make up. Knowing the mean things that were said, jobs or lack of jobs that made finances tight, hanging out with friends, just to name a few, are hard to ignore once the door is opened and the truth is revealed.

When you have a loving and attentive husband, it is unacceptable to see your daughter with one that is not. If you have had a previous relationship or marriage where abuse or neglect was present, it becomes unbearable, for we know what Scripture tells us about how a husband is to treat his wife.

> And you husbands must love your wives with the same love Christ showed the church. He gave up his life for her to make her holy and clean, washed by baptism and God's word. He did this to present her to himself as a glorious church without a spot or wrinkle or any other blemish. Instead, she will be holy and without fault. In the same way, husbands ought to love their wives as they love their own bodies. For a man is actually loving himself when he loves his wife.
>
> Ephesians 5:25–28 (NLT)

If there is actually physical, emotional, or mental abuse, you must speak up, get professional assistance, and be greatly involved to remove your child from the dangerous situation. If the problem is more of not living up to expectations, letting everyone down, or a lack of maturity level, then you may have to stop being your daughter's shoulder. Help her find a pastor or Christian counselor to talk to. Sons-in-law are not normally combative, but they can control the narrative if they feel they are being the focus of conversations.

## The Father-Son-in-law Relationship

This relationship usually is uneventful unless there is some sort of abuse, neglect, or other types of conduct that can cause harm, injury, mental or physical pain, or financial hardships toward a daughter by her husband, and the father knows about it. Protection toward his child will almost always result in the deterioration of the relationship with the person causing the harm or injustice.

The importance of a father being willing to give advice and the son-in-law willing to listen and take the advice is found in Exodus 18:13–22; 24 (NLT):

> The next day, Moses sat as usual to hear the people's complaints against each other. They were lined up in front of him from morning till evening.
>
> When Moses' father-in-law saw all that Moses was doing for the people, he said, "Why are you trying to do all this alone? The people have been standing here all day to get your help."
>
> Moses replied," Well, the people come to me to seek God's guidance. When an argument arises, I am the one who settles the case. I inform the people of God's decisions and teach them his laws and instructions."

"This is not good!" his father-in-law exclaimed. "You're going to wear yourself out—and the people, too. This job is too heavy a burden for you to handle all by yourself. Now let me give you a word of advice, and may God be with you. You should continue to be the people's representative before God, bringing him their questions to be decided. You should tell them God's decisions, teach them God's laws and instructions, and show them how to conduct their lives. But find some capable, honest men who fear God and hate bribes. Appoint them as judges over groups of one thousand, one hundred, fifty, and ten. These men can serve the people, resolving all ordinary cases..."

Moses listened to his father-in-law's advice and followed his suggestion.

The relationship between Moses and Jethro was respectful, honorable, and included God's blessing on the advice. The advice reflected Jethro's concern for Moses and the people he counseled.

Today's advice from one generation to another is often less well-received, but that doesn't mean it shouldn't be done. If you realize resentment or a spirit of offense occurs, even when the advice or guidance is given with only the best of intentions and experience, step away silently and with your head held high.

This advice is hard for me personally. Many years ago, I made a solemn promise that I would never, to the best of my ability, have to say, "I wish I had said something." I did not want to find out someone was in the hospital and think, *I wish I had said something*; I did not want to face the parents of a teen in jail and think, *I wish I had said something*, and I did not want to attend a funeral and through tears think "I wish I had said something."

This means I must learn discernment between those things that can just be learned by trial and error, success and failure, and those things that are critical and urgent. In matters of physical and mental safety, legal jeopardy, and salvation, especially salvation, I will speak up. Put up a brick wall, and I will climb it and yell from the top. But I will not keep quiet and think, *I wish I had said something*. And that is because of Love, in its purest form.

**Silently and Privately, between You and God**

Looking at and analyzing your relationship today with your adult child, are there any additional criteria that makes your situation different than those addressed?

_____

_____

_____

_____

_____

Are there any things that do not apply to you or that are of greater consequence than they should be?

_____

_____

_____

_____

_____

# Looking in the Mirror

To be fair, daughters and sons can have some legitimate complaints about their parents. Sometimes we just weren't there when we were needed. Sometimes we were there too much. A child does not recognize that their parents are just imperfect humans and that raising a child is a learn-as-you-go process with no instruction manual. Resentment can build up if a child sees his parents as "good at everything," such as career, homemaking, and handyman skills. They think they will never live up to the high bar you have set in their mind. Sometimes, they think you had other priorities over them, such as careers, social life, or addictions. This resentment leaves them feeling you didn't care and you didn't get involved in their growth.

The sad truth is, as a society, we have honestly failed to stand our ground on the important basics of family and faith as we were lulled into modern conveniences.

You see, studies have shown that anything diminished in one generation is further diminished in the next and eventually disappears. For example, the simple task of everyone sitting around the dinner table. Before 1952, most families gathered in the dining room or kitchen and sat sharing a meal and conversation. Then, the invention of the TV tray and, in 1953, the frozen TV dinner. Meals shifted to the den or living room or both if the family had two televisions. Conversation over the next generation was replaced by the script of *Bonanza*, *Wonderful World of Disney*, or the antics of *I Love Lucy*. Today, many meals are consumed in the car or dropped off by a delivery driver and taken to different corners of the home. Conversation between family members is not the only thing lost in this shift. Conversations with God through the blessing of the meal, and then bedtime prayers, Sunday school, church services have all taken a back seat to whatever is "more urgent" or "more entertaining."

Whether too much or too little or even somewhere in the middle, there will be times in every parent-child relationship when things seem to fall apart, and you are not sure if they will ever be repaired.

This is a good time for self-reflection. The hardest thing for us to do is recognize what we are doing wrong when we think our intentions were only to be supportive and loving.

None of us know our faults. Forgive me when
I sin without knowing it.

Psalm 19:12 (CEV)

Recognizing that you are too involved is hard. If you
didn't have someone around to do little things for you,
you tend to want to do those little things for your grown
kids. It never enters your mind that they will think you
are criticizing them if you wash the dishes while watching grandkids. You are just remembering how it felt to
come home from work and have to do dishes instead of
reading a story to your little one, and you want to give
that gift of time to your daughter-in-law.

The little things you just naturally do, the little things
can blow up like an unexpected arsenal of resentment
and bitterness. These unknown offenses are the hardest
to comprehend, and it is so hard to recognize your role
in the conflict with your children when your intentions
are to be helpful, protective, and encouraging.

It hurts when these intentions are taken as invasive,
smothering, and offensive. But recognize them, you
must. And then work on how to react to the misunderstandings and reactions you have incurred thus far.

My dear brothers and sisters, be quick to listen, slow to speak, and slow to get angry. Your

anger can never make things right in God's sight.

James 1:19–20 (NLT)

Add to this scripture, "Slow, very, very slow to become hurt and upset." But remember the fig tree. Don't give up: One more hour...one more day...one more year.

## Silently and Privately, between You and God

What are the legitimate complaints you recognize that your adult child could have against you?

_____

_____

_____

What were your intentions or reasons behind your actions or inactions that these complaints come from?

_____

_____

_____

In what areas of your family life, prior to adulthood for your children, do you feel were neglected or that took a back seat to other, less important things?

_____

_____

_____

What specific things are you surprised to find out were taken as offensive to your adult child that you did with pure good intentions?

_____

_____

_____

How are you reacting to those discoveries and how can you alter your behaviors or actions to "lessen this offense" without compromising your values or lessen your objective of securing your child's relationship with our Savior, Jesus Christ?

_____

_____

_____

_____

# The Longest Journey Starts with the First Step

**Step 1:** Breathe. Take a moment to take a deep breath. Calm your heart, your mind, your body. Nothing is accomplished when you run on pure adrenaline and emotion. Get centered so you can hear a Word from God.

> Be still, and know that I am God!
>
> Psalm 46:10 (NLT)

**Step 2:** Pray. Open your heart and talk to God with full disclosure, honesty, and sincerity. He already knows what is in your heart, what you need, and what you want. But you have to work on a personal relationship with God by being open and honest with yourself, which comes through prayer.

> Rejoice always, pray without ceasing, give
> thanks in all circumstances; for this is the will
> of God in Christ Jesus for you.
>
> 1 Thessalonians 5:16–18 (ESV)

**Step 3:** Live to please God. You may never please your children, and even though you invest time, energy, prayer, and tears into your relationship with them, you cannot let it consume you. In everything you do, from this day forward, examine your motives. It is a good and natural part of life for a parent to want to spend time with children and grandchildren, watching them succeed and grow. But when your relationship with your adult children and their families becomes an obsession, all you can think about, and if your emotions are being tied up in knots with every word said, what is your motive? For you to be loved and cared for, or for them to live a life that honors the Kingdom.

> For we speak as messengers who have been
> approved by God to be entrusted with the
> Good News. Our purpose is to please God, not
> people. He is the one who examines the mo-
> tives of our hearts.
>
> 1 Thessalonians 2:4 (NLT)

**Step 4:** Forgive. The most difficult and most necessary thing you could ever possibly do is forgive. Forgive the eye rolls, the snappy comebacks, the unanswered phone calls. Forgive the name-calling, forgive empty chairs at the table, forgive the words said under their breath. Forgive every transgression, slight and hurt. Say it, write it, show it.

> Then Peter came to him and asked, "Lord, how often should I forgive someone who sins against me? Seven times?"
> "No, not seven times," Jesus replied, "but seventy times seven!"
>
> Matthew 18:21–22 (NLT)

Don't keep count of the number, don't keep track, don't make mental notes, just forgive. The KJV of the Bible uses the word "forgive" ninety-five times. There is no greater gift that we have than the ability to forgive someone. It is a gift for them and a gift for us. Use the gift.

Then, *forgive yourself*. Forgive every eye roll, snappy comeback, and unanswered phone call. Forgive yourself for every name called, every empty chair at the table, and words said under your breath. Forgive yourself. Say it, write it, show it. Apologize for your part in the battle.

> So if you are standing before the altar in the Temple, offering a sacrifice to God, and you

suddenly remember that someone has something against you, leave your sacrifice there beside the altar. Go and be reconciled to that person. Then come and offer your sacrifice to God. Come to terms quickly with your enemy before it is too late...

Matthew 5:23–25 (NLT)

Forgiveness gives peace. Forgiveness does not mean everything will be fine. It does not mean you won't have a repeat what you just forgave. It does not mean you will forget, but you can have peace. Peace is a treasure you want to hold onto. Don't let anyone steal it. Peace is obtained through a close relationship with God, with Jesus, with the Holy Spirit. If you are filled with bitterness, with sorrow, with hurts, and with memories of everything done and said, there is no room for the peace and joy that awaits you. Forgive, just forgive.

And do not bring sorrow to God's Holy Spirit by the way you live. Remember, he is the one who has identified you as his own, guaranteeing that you will be saved on the day of redemption. Get rid of all bitterness, rage, anger, harsh words, and slander, as well as all types of malicious behavior. Instead, be kind to each other, tenderhearted, forgiving one

another, just as God through Christ has forgiven you.

Ephesians 4:30–32 (NLT)

### Silently and Privately, between You and God

Where is your place of peace and prayer? Find or develop a place in your home or yard that you can go to daily to be *still, pray, listen and breathe*. The spot I meet with God daily is_____

_____

Write down on a separate sheet of paper or on a piece of wood the things you need to forgive. All the words said, all the thoughts, all the things that make you angry or make your heart heavy. Write down all the names of those you need to forgive (include your own name). Take your time. Make sure you have covered it all.

Pray over this list. Read it out loud to the Lord. Then safely find a place you can burn it, cast it into moving water, or bury it so deep it will never be found. Let it go...let the Holy Spirit fill your heart with peace and joy. When you have done the above, write forgiven on this line: _____

# When to Walk and When to Run, and in What Direction

Don't worry—I am with you. Don't be afraid—
I am your God. I will make you strong and
help you. I will support you with my right
hand that brings victory.

Isaiah 41:10 (ERV)

We have pretty much established that now is the time to choose between being the eggshell walking, just going along with anything, keeping your mouth shut, and your prayers to yourself kind of parent.

*Or*

A King Solomon (Proverbs) advice-giving; whole armor of God wearing (Ephesians 6:10–18); manifestly 'til the walls are shaking and the chains fall off praying (Acts 25–26), kind of parent.

If you choose door number one, you can probably be guaranteed holidays with family: Lukewarm but civil conversations about nothing that matters, family photos, invitations to this and that, and a deep sense of something missing. Walking on eggshells may be the right answer for you in the short term. If going along to get along for a while is the best way to keep in contact with your adult children during a "rough patch" or time of growth or the only way to keep in a close relationship with your grandchildren, then this is an option you may have to live with.

These are the times when you can recognize that the deterioration in your relationship is the result of normal everyday life items. Choices that to them make sense, even when they don't make sense. In other words, although you really don't get why your adult child (including your children, stepchildren, and their spouses) would choose to react the way they are, you can look at it and see who or what has influenced them, who they are trying to impress, suppress, or address. You can see their point of view, even when it is clearly out of focus. With prayer, patience, an adjustment in your reactions, there is a light—however dim—within view.

Additionally, developing a relationship with young grandchildren is important. When adult children infer that they will withhold visits or even harder, when you have been involved daily in their lives, and the possibility of that going away happens, you sometimes must bite the bullet and put on your egg-walking shoes. Make the most of every opportunity to fill them up with love, stories about your family, about Jesus, and making sure giggles and warm cookies are what their memories and opinions will be made up of in case things go wrong later.

> A good person leaves an inheritance for their
> children's children...
>
> Proverbs 13:22 (NIV)

A financial inheritance is not all you give your children's children. You leave them a legacy of character, blessings, beliefs, habits, and love. Every day should be an investment of what your grandchildren will receive as their inheritance from you. If that means a few eggshells on the floor and a bit of lip on occasion, then let it be temporarily. Prayers will be your weapon and your strength.

> And let us not grow weary of doing good, for
> in due season we will reap, if we do not give
> up.
>
> Galatians 6:9 (ESV)

If you choose door number two, you have recognized that your relationship is at a point of needing serious attention. The spiral is leading to a place where mental, physical, or spiritual well-being is deteriorating, and time appears to be of the essence. At this point, you must leave door number one slightly ajar and be ready to identify when your reactions will be that of a nurturer and when it will be that of a warrior. Being a nurturer does not mean you are a doormat. You do not ever permit yourself to be spoken to in a way that is demeaning or insulting. Your children have a God-given obligation to treat you with honor. Honor is to choose love over hatred, harmony over discord, gratitude over bitterness, and live over the death of a relationship.

> Children, obey your parents because you belong to the Lord, for this is the right thing to do. Honor your father and mother. This is the first of the Ten Commands that ends with a promise. And this is the promise: If you honor your father and mother, you will live a long life, full of blessings.
>
> Ephesians 6:1–3 (NLT)

On the other hand, you are never to be a brick wall, unmoving and uncaring.

And now a word to you fathers. Don't make your children angry by the way you treat them.

Rather bring them up with the discipline and
instruction approved by the Lord.

Ephesians 6:4 (NLT)

For you know that we dealt with each of you as
a father deals with his own children, encouraging, comforting, and urging you to live lives
worthy of God, who calls you to his kingdom
and glory.

1 Thessalonians 2:11–12 (NIV)

So, let's get the conversations started again, even if
they will at times be taken and received as an offense.

But there are times when you realize that something
bigger is happening. Nothing makes sense, and you
cannot find any reasonable or tangible explanation for
the major change. It may involve an actual change in
personality, responses, facial expressions, or daily rou-
tines. Suddenly chaos is evident, and it is not normal
chaos. The Leviathan spirit is often used by the enemy
to infiltrate family relationships or marriages and to
create confusion. Words are twisted and used to cause
misunderstandings. In a normal conversation, what is
said is completely different from what someone hears.
Pride and fear become a part of everything. A lack of
motivation and an acceptance of just giving up is present and Covenant breaking. Walking away from prom-

ises is accepted without effort to work on an issue, whether actual or perceived.

This is the time to swing door number two wide open. Put on your full armor and become a prayer warrior. Two basic things to recognize: demons exist, and they can influence and oppress people. Spirits like Leviathan (chaos, misunderstandings, deceit) and Jezebel (promiscuity, wickedness) are allowed in through doors opened, often innocently, and under the cover of entertainment or friendships.

The one major thing to remember, to know, to declare with every ounce of your mind, body, and soul is God is Greater.

If you recognize that the root cause of the problem is one that requires spiritual warfare, then you must keep your eyes on the cross and your direction running toward the Kingdom. At this time, you must protect yourself from falling into the traps that will also drag you into the deceptions. Recognize that you are in this battle for your children and their children and their children. You must not surrender, and you must fight the spiritual battle. God is Greater, and His will is what you declare and fight for.

## Silently and Privately, between You and God

Which "door" do you feel God is leading you to choose as to your approach to healing with your adult child today?

_____

_____

_____

How do you think you will protect your heart if you must temporarily walk away from what is becoming a bad situation with your adult children and when will you know it is time to try again?

_____

_____

_____

Are you spiritually prepared to fight the fight if you are led to believe there is more influencing your adult child than can be understood and explained?

_____

_____

_____

# Remaining Strong, Together

Two people can accomplish more than twice as much as one; they get a better return for their labor. If one person falls, the other can reach out and help. But people who are alone when they fall are in real trouble. And on a cold night, two under the same blanket can gain warmth from each other. But how can one be warm alone? A person standing alone can be attacked and defeated, but two can stand back-to-back and conquer. Three are even better, for a triple-braided cord is not easily broken.

Ecclesiastes 4:9–12 (NLT)

This is not an easy path that you are going down. Married couples must trust each other with honesty and communication. One of you alone cannot fix the problem, and you should not dismiss one another's feelings if you have not experienced the same slights or behaviors from your children. Remember, from about the age of one, children learn how to play one parent against the other. Mom says, "No cookies," and Dad gives me a cookie, and their skills have only improved over the years.

If you don't have a husband or wife to pick you up, share a blanket or stand back-to-back, go to that person who has over the years proven to be "your person." Or maybe you have developed a bond with your Bible study or discipleship group at church, and your pastor is always one to seek council from. Share what you are going through with them and remember what Jesus told the apostles:

> Again, truly I tell you that if two of you on earth agree about anything they ask for, it will be done for them by my Father in heaven. For where two or three gather in my name, there am I with them.
>
> Matthew 18:19–20 (NIV)

This journey of prayer, witness, reconciliation, and redemption is a team effort.

Listen, my son, to your father's instruction
and do not forsake your mother's teaching.

Proverbs 1:8 (NIV)

Fathers have been given specific responsibilities
throughout Scripture. They are to direct their children,
their households to do what is right and just. When a
man is boldly given instruction on leading his children,
no matter what their age, to live lives worthy of God, it
is hard to be sure exactly how to do that. The empha-
sis has to be to carefully lead, not forcefully pull them
along.

Listen, my son, accept what I say, and the
years of your life will be many. I instruct you
in the way of wisdom and lead you along
straight paths.

Proverbs 4:10–11 (NIV)

For I have chosen him, so that he will direct
his children and his household after him to
keep the way of the Lord by doing what is right
and just, so that the Lord will bring about for
Abraham what he has promised him.

Genesis 18:19 (NIV)

Do what is right and just. Are you? Am I? Do we undertake all the things that would completely turn our relationships around? Probably not because we as parents are human. With flaws, failures, baggage, sins, and inequities, we live our lives, trying to do the best we can and failing miserably.

This means we must stop seeing life in the negative. Stop focusing on what has happened and start imagining what will happen with the guidance of Scripture.

> Finally, brothers and sisters, whatever is true, whatever is noble, whatever is right, whatever is pure, whatever is lovely, whatever is admirable—if anything is excellent or praiseworthy—think about such things. Whatever you have learned or received or heard from me, or seen in me—put into practice...
> Philippians 4:8–9 (NIV)

You must make every effort to see results. This is not the time to be distracted or lazy. If your children are close, put down your phone and talk. If they are far away, pick up your phone and talk.

They may not want to hear what you are saying, and if that is the case, Talk to the Holy Spirit. He will be your advocate and can do more to open their eyes to see and open their ears to hear than anything you can say or do.

It is so much easier to have started this when they were young. If you missed the opportunity to do this with your children, do it with your grandchildren. But in the grand scheme of things, it is never too late to teach your children about God, about all the things we know we are to do.

> Love the Lord your God with all your heart and with all your soul and with all your strength. Take to heart these words that I give you to-day. Repeat them to your children. Talk about them when you're at home or away, when you lie down or get up. Write them down, and tie them around your wrist, and wear them as headbands as a reminder. Write them down on the doorframes of your houses and on your gates.
>
> Deuteronomy 6:5–9 (GW)

If you have already done these things, do them again. If you have left gaps, fill them in. If you never got started, get started.

## Privately and Silently, between You and God

Have you had an open, honest conversation with your spouse, or supportive friend relaying how you are being treated, feeling, responding and what your goals are?

_____

_____

_____

_____

# Prayer Time (2)

*Dearest Heavenly Father,*

*We are here as parents; with a love you understand and support for those we call our children. Our needs and desires for close relationships with them are so small in relation to our needs and desires for them to have a close relationship with you. We are here praying for guidance and opportunities to lead them toward you. We are here praying for wisdom and understanding. We are here praying for unity in our families under Christ.*

*Lord, Paul asked for spiritual wisdom to be granted to your children in the church at Ephesus. We are here asking the same for our children, the children you gave us to love and cherish and raise according to your plan. We have failed in so many ways, but our request is the same as Paul's: open the eyes of their hearts and let the light of your truth flood in. Shine your light on the hope you are calling them to embrace. Reveal to them the glorious riches you are preparing as their inheritance.*

*As the walls between the Gentiles and Jews were torn down and they were made one through Christ, we pray that the walls between any member of our families be removed and replaced with a foundation to build our households upon with Christ Jesus as the cornerstone.*

*In Jesus' Most Holy Name,*
*Amen.*

But you, take courage! Do not let your hands be weak, for your work shall be rewarded.

2 Chronicles 15:7 (ESV)

# Aha Moment

If you take away only one thing from this book, let it be this:

You can *give* with the best of intentions, with love, with experience, and with blessings. How a person *receives* that gift is totally, completely, and solely their choice and responsibility.

Understanding this was my Aha moment. That sudden realization that I did not have any control over how another person thinks and reacts. You see, having already gone through tough times with my older children, I really thought I had this parenting thing down pat. Then suddenly, one day, the floor was once again filled with eggshells, and walls of bitterness and tears replaced open arms and laughter. Everything said was taken as an offense, and the words Jesus spoke in Luke 12:52–53 were again being used by the enemy to separate families, my family, "From now on, families will be split apart, three in favor of me, and two against—or the other way around. There will be a division between father and son, mother and daughter, mother-in-law, and daughter-in-law" (NLT).

So, silently and privately, I mourned for my children. The feelings of failure, confusion, fear, anger, incompetence, and the voice of Satan whispering in my ear, "You don't deserve a family that loves you," came flooding in from all the years before.

But, and this is a big but, the words of Joseph to his brothers were once again proven true. "As far as I am concerned, God turned into good what you meant for evil" (Genesis 50:20).

An unexpected phone call; the memory of a book started years earlier. Breathe, pray, live to please God, write.

My prayer is that all of us will soon witness a happy ending to this difficult journey we are traveling. But now you know, I know, that we are not traveling alone. There is no shame in whatever path we decide to take, as long as we keep our eye on the cross.

And every day, remember the fig tree: Don't give up... one more hour, one more day, one more year.

### Silently and Privately, between You and God

Use this journaling page to:
- Write down scripture that you need to read daily
- Write down a prayer to repeat every day
- Write down your blessings, so they don't get overshadowed by trials

_____

_____

_____

_____

_____

_____

_____

_____

_____

_____

_____

_____

_____

_____

_____

_____

_____

# About the Author

Brenda Brittain is best described as a proud Texas woman, devoted wife, mother, grandmother, home-maker, business owner, and most importantly, a Christian. Blessed to be a member of Foundation Christian Ministries in Bastrop, Texas, she is an active disciple-maker and sister-in-Christ. Her first book, *The Seven Courses of Christianity*, was a thought-provoking journey through the progression of faith using the image of a seven-course meal. Traveling and teaching this book to many churches included serving each course to partici-pants' real hands-on teaching. Her next book was in-spired by a youth group she led as Director of Christian Education at First United Methodist Church in Elgin, Texas. Using the *Minute to Win It* game both literally and figuratively, young Christians—of all ages—learn as they journey with Paul and walk in the footsteps of Jesus.

Her latest book, *The Mourning of Our Children*, is a different type of journey. One many parents of healthy, successful, popular, and for reasons indescribable, very distant adult children are traveling, but not alone.

CPSIA information can be obtained
at www.ICGtesting.com
Printed in the USA
LVHW080710010722
722487LV00011B/238

9 781685 566074